T0209568

An experience with God expressed in words but still does not do Him justice. The expression of His greatness is limited as it passes through this vessel, but may these words help draw you closer to encounter the greatness of our Father, our Lord and Saviour Jesus Christ.

Diary with the Lord

Book of Poems

Prudence Edwards

WESTBOW
P R E S S®
A DIVISION OF THOMAS NELSON
& ZONDERVAN

WestBow Press books may be ordered through booksellers or by contacting:

WestBow Press
A Division of Thomas Nelson & Zondervan
1663 Liberty Drive
Bloomington, IN 47403
www.westbowpress.com
1 (866) 928-1240

Photo credit: Prudence Edwards
Scenery: Providenciales, Turks and Caicos Islands

ISBN: 978-1-9736-5270-0 (sc)
ISBN: 978-1-9736-5271-7 (e)

Library of Congress Control Number: 2019901456

Print information available on the last page.

WestBow Press rev. date: 04/24/2019

Contents

Acknowledgements

A very big thank-you to Pastor Roy Rampersaud. He was the first person who told me I should publish, and over the years, consistently kept encouraging me. I needed the encouragement and the reminders.

A heartfelt thank-you to other friends and family members who have taken time out to read work I have shared and provided feedback. I appreciated it deeply and will always be grateful.

With a humble heart, I thank the Holy Spirit for so often nudging me and reminding me that God expects us to use our talents.

May lives be blessed.

Introduction

Diary with the Lord is mainly a book of poems and was inspired by my own personal experience with the Lord Almighty. Even though it touches on some of my lowest points during my walk with Christ, it mainly focuses on a period of my life when my faith was tested but I was determined to trust God, with His help.

Serving God was what I was created for, and I was at my most comfortable, most confident, and happiest when I was serving the Creator.

It is my desire that this book serves as an encouragement and helps towards strengthening your faith in God.

Chapter 1

Testimonials

In the Deepest Part of Me

I felt it in my heart, in the deepest part of me,
that part logic could not penetrate.
In the deepest recess I kept it.
They called me a fool, they mocked, they said I was just
dreaming.
But I refused to budge.
Because I felt it in my heart, in the deepest part of me,
where human reasoning couldn't reach.

Years came, years passed, but I held on.
I flirted with danger, flirted with sin to assuage the desire
within.
But it stayed in the deepest part of me; Your promise I felt.

More years passed, and the doubts crept in.
But Lord, You reminded me of the promise You made in
the deepest part of me.
I sought Your face, and You reassured me with grace.
I held on to the promise You made so many years before.
I felt it in my heart, in the deepest part of me, where
human philosophy couldn't touch.

The year came, and I sought Your face once again
with a request for a vision of the promise You made so
many years ago.

Despite my questions, I did not recognize Your answer.
Like a loving Father, You repeated, giving me a new
revelation.
There were giants on my land,

huge and imposing, impossible to move.
But I knew the giants had to go.

Weeks turned into months, with giants occupying my
Promised Land.
I cried on my knees; I fought by faith, knowing that
someday all the giants had to go. They will be dead.

I now stand with joy in my heart that I believed.
The supernatural blessings I received because I believed
in the deepest part of my heart, where human mockery
could not change.
Where the devil's schemes could not meet.

The Lord countered the giants.
I inherited His promise, a land flowing with milk and
honey, where I will now dwell.

Keep that promise in your heart, in the deepest part of
you. Keep the promise in your heart, in the deepest part
of you.

Standing on the Brink

Tears rolling down my cheeks.
Despair a thick fog, enclosing me in its darkness.
Enveloped by trouble, losing air,
Gasping for breath, clawing at straws,
Meeting my fate,
Screaming my pain.
It is time I jump.

But then I heard that still, small voice: "Don't!"
Powerful in its intensity,
Soothing and calm.
Comforting in its love,
Enveloping me in peace.
It just can't be real.

The voice spoke again: "Remember."
And I did.
Ignoring the darkness clawing at my soul,
I remember, *If I make my bed in hell, He's there.*
I turned to the still, small voice and cried, "Help me!"
And He did!
Today, I can testify, "He saved me!"
I am now standing on solid rock,
My death a distant memory.

*I*t Hurts, but I Wait

Lord, I bare my soul to You.
I bare my thoughts and my feelings, my pains and my hurts.

When You say it is mine, I'm confused when I do not receive it.
I am hurt that it hurts.

My desire to possess is great; You did say it is mine.
Then it is mine! I cannot release my hold.
I want it! I desire it! I need it!
"Then why the long wait?" I ask.
I have done all that You have asked.
What more is there for me to do?
I waited as You have instructed.

Yes, Lord, it hurts that it hurts when it is mine.
It belongs to me; You said it is mine.
I may not understand why it hurts, but I trust in You, Lord.
I wait on You, Lord, to bring it all to pass.
I hold onto Your promise; I hold tight to the hope.

My faith is intact because I know
You will bring it to pass,
Your promise of peace, joy, compassion, love, blessings, and fulfilment.
I wait on You, Lord.
I wait on You, Lord, the tidal wave of Your grace,
The fulfilment of Your promise.

The Pit a Ladder

The pit is just a ladder to my next destination.
It is dark, it is deep; I cannot see the top.
There is no light within.
It is so small; I'm losing air.
I'm drowning in despair,
Crying in my pain.
But this pit is just a ladder to my next destination.

At last, light is here!
I am rescued from the dark.
Rejoicing in the Lord,
Hallelujah, I am free!

But salvation is snatched again
As I am now sold as a slave.
I don't understand it, Lord.
You said I'll be king, to rule in dignity.
Here I am, sinking even deeper
To the bottom of the ladder.
But this pit is just a ladder to my next destination.

I am now gaining hope
As head of my master's household.
It's not freedom,
But I am comforted.
Some dignity has been restored.
With diligence and grace, I serve,
Praying I am fulfilling my Father's will.
This pit is just a ladder to my next destination.

There is a turn for the worse
I'm falsely accused,
Thrown in jail.
Is this it?
Shackled in a dungeon,
Looked at with scorn,
Death sentencing pending
For doing what the Lord laid on my heart.

Lord, what have I done wrong?
He says, "This pit is just a ladder to your next destination.
Royalty you are, and I am looking over you.
I am monitoring the temperature
To elevate you as pure gold,
Tried, tested, and perfected."

So, I thank You, Lord,
As this pit is just a ladder
toward my final destination.
I know in my heart
My destiny is sure!

*C*onversation with My God

ME. Lord, I trust You. I believe in Your promise. I wait on You. But Lord, why do I have to wait so long?

THE LORD. I'm building your faith and developing patience.

ME. OK, Lord, I submit to You.
But Lord, this waiting is so hard. I need Your comfort through the wait.

THE LORD. You have it!
(*I then feel His love comforting me.*)

ME. Lord, thank You! I'm so grateful that everything that concerns me You care about.
(*I'm now happily smiling in my Father's arms.*)

ME. Lord, this wait…

THE LORD. Trust Me.

ME. I'm trusting You, Lord.

ME. Lord, the wait is so painful. How much longer?

THE LORD.   (SILENCE)

ME.   Lord?

THE LORD.   Trust Me.

ME.   OK, Lord, I trust You.
           Lord, if I didn't believe in Your promises
           and didn't know that You honour Your
           Word above Your name, I would have given
           up a long time ago. It's so painful. The
           enemy's hits are painful. But I'm trusting
           You, Lord, looking forward to my reward.
           It's going to be glorious, I know.

THE LORD.   Yes, it will. As King, Author, and Creator,
           I give good gifts.
           (*I'm comforted and excited about my reward.*)

ME.   But Lord, how are You going to get it done?
           Don't answer that! Faith doesn't need
           details. Your ways are far above mine. I
           thank You, Lord.

           (TIME PASSES)

THE LORD.   Victory is today.

ME.   Thank You, Lord. I receive it!

9

THE LORD.   A shift is coming in your life. I have more than enough for you if you hold on.

ME.   Thank You, Lord. Thank You, Lord.
(*I'm mentally dancing on the ceiling.*)

(TIME PASSES)

ME   Lord, I'm hurting. The enemy's jab was painful. Please revenge me, Lord, as You said, "Vengeance is Mine."

THE LORD.   I'm a God of justice. I will.

ME.   I'm looking forward to it. I'm excited to say, "See what my God has done. See that my God is real. Yes, my God always keeps His promises. My God is awesome."

THE LORD.   Those who wait on Me will mount up with wings like eagles. They will receive what I have promised.

ME.   I worship You, Lord.

I AM NOW STANDING ON HIS WORD.
I WILL NOT BE MOVED.

Chapter 2

Love Letters, My Worship

My God and I

The grace of God is like an addiction.
Having His presence, His love, hearing His Word,
Food to my soul,
Breath to my being,
Flesh to my bone.
I need Him.
He revives me,
Gives me comfort, gives me strength,
Loves me when I'm broken,
Loved me when I was lost,
Faithful through my unfaithfulness,
Keeps me safe,
Shelters me from life's storms.

I'm so grateful to You, Lord.
I'm emotionally stable because of You.
Yes, Lord,
I'm sane because You kept me through it all.

I can rejoice,
I can jump for joy,
I can sing with mirth,
I can dance as if there are no cares
Because You care for me.
With You, I am sheltered in my Father's care.

Just You, Lord

Lord, I love You, and I trust You.
My world may be collapsing all around,
but once I have You, that's all that matters.
Just You and me, Lord.
Through it all, just You and me.
With You here with me, I can handle the storms.

My needs, my desires, my prayers, my requests—they no
longer matter.
What matters is that You are here with me
in my every breath.

I need You in every step.

It is all temporal—only You, Lord.
Eternity with You is all I need.
You, Lord—that is all I need.

So, I submit myself to You.
Forgetting all else—just You, Lord.
That's all; that's all I need.

Who You Are

You are awesome.
You are great.
Only You are good.
You are wisdom.
You are perfection.
You are the beginning and the end.
You are my God.

You are the Creator.
You are my Father.
You are my friend and my confidant.
You stick closer than a brother.
You are Ruler and King.
You are my God!

You are my healer.
You are my protector.
You are my provider,
My fortress, my haven.
You are my righteousness.
You are my peace.
You are my God!

You are majestic.
You are beautiful.
You are love.
You are the great I Am.
You are God.

*O*h, Lord, You Are Beautiful

Lord, I cannot stand before You.
When I stare into the beauty of who You are,
My knees buckle and my heart palpitates.
My entire being is on pause when I encounter Your grace.

I feel death knocking at my door when I gaze upon You,
falling deep in Your embrace.
A death I welcome, a sweet death to experience the beauty
of You.

Flesh and bone won't do; I need more of You.
I need to experience that beauty that peeks through when
I worship You.

I need to hear Your voice and feel Your love in everything
I do.

My physical man cannot comprehend,
Cannot sustain the beauty of You.
My heart bursts at how awesome You are.
Oh, Lord, You are beautiful!

But beautiful is inadequate to express Your depth.
What word can there be to describe the Creator of all
things,
the Being that is self-existing, that has no beginning and
no end?
What word describes the power that has no limit?

What word can explain Your awesomeness,
Your depths and Your heights?

So, I say, hallelujah to praise and honour the I Am,
The King of kings and Lord of lords, the only God.

Oh, Lord, hallelujah, I worship You.

My Choice of Drug

Oh, how I need You.
Every day I need You.
Every waking hour, I need You.
When I wake, I reach for You,
Knowing You are right there,
Never, ever far away.

I wake during the night and call Your name, Jehovah …
and You answer me by name.
You are always here, with outstretched arms ready to
listen to my pains,
Soothing me in my despair.

When I call on You during the day,
You say, "Here I am."

Father, You are that drug I am addicted to,
And no cost I paid,
No negative effect I bear.
You showed me paradise on earth.
You showed me I can be high and out of this world.
Yes, with You, I experience euphoria and real supernatural
power.
I'm floating beyond the present, beyond the now.
I'm in a different realm far above clouds.
I am happily high on You.

Enjoying the safety of Your touch,
loving the taste of You.
Oh, friends, taste and see that the Lord is good.
Enjoy the intoxicating effect of His love.
My God, my Father, my choice of drug.

Chapter 3

Warfare

War

The devil is camping, strategising against me …
Planning demonic schemes to frustrate, hurt, and kill me.
He wants to delay the plan of God in my life…
he wants to break me.
But I stand in the authority God had given me.

I trample on every attack.
Every scheme I renounce!
I storm the gate of hell …
I storm the atmosphere …
I storm the devil's camp.

It is war!

I war in confidence, I war in righteous anger…
I defeat the defeated enemy.

I set his plans on fire.
I burn them with the blood of the Lamb.

It is war!

I war in the spirit, I war on my knees.
I war with no fear.
I am a soldier in the Lord's camp.
I war because the victory has already been won.

I strapped on my armour in preparation for war,
But I war in silence, I war in peace, I war in love.
I war in my stillness, because God is fighting for me.

I Fight!

What God has given me, I fight to have, to keep.
I fight for His perfect will.
I fight with grace.
With a conquering spirit, I fight!

I fight on my knees in prayer.
I fight with praise.
I fight with thanksgiving.
I decree, declare, proclaim, and exclaim about the promises of God,
until I possess them all.

Yes, I fight. I am fighting with grace.

I fight with authority, sealed by the precious blood of the Lamb.
Yes, I fight in agreement with my Saviour and King.
I fight with the warring angels.
I fight on the winning team.
I fight with grace.

I fight with weapons that are sharp and clean, perfectly fitted in place—
My helmet of salvation,
My breastplate of righteousness.
My loins, gird about with truth.
My feet with peace.
Wielding the sword of the Spirit—the Word of God.
With my shield of faith, warding off the enemy's darts.

I fight with grace!

My fight is not carnal.
My fight is not against flesh.
I fight against the devil,
Against imaginations, strongholds, and those things that
exalt against the knowledge of God.

I fight because I know who I am.
I fight to win, even though I have already won.
I fight in confidence!
I fight with no fear!
I am fighting with grace.

$\mathcal{I}$ Declare

I declare! I declare!
I will scream it from the mountaintop, I declare!
A wretch like me, God has given authority to declare.
So yes! I make my declaration on the promises God made.

I scream it out, I declare!
I declare, I am the head!
You can follow me, because I will lead you to Christ.
I was born into the army of God,
It is written in my DNA
and sealed by the blood of the Lamb,
I will not be forgotten—
my name is seared into the palm of my Father's hand.

So yes! I declare! I declare!
I declare, no weapon formed against me shall prosper,
As it is my inheritance from the King—
the King of kings, my God.

Are you going to challenge me?
Just know you will be fighting royalty, a child of the King.
You will lose!
This is a fixed fight.
My victory has already been decided.
I declare!

I declare! I declare!
There is healing in my body,
There is healing in my spirit,
There is healing in my mind

Because by His stripes, I am healed.
He was bruised for my iniquity.
He was chastised for my peace.
I am healed and I am set apart.
I declare!

As He took the wounds for my transgression,
I have been declared not guilty, for He took my place.
He stood in the gap, releasing me from my sins.
I stand because of grace and say with authority,

I declare!

Power in Words

Be careful what you say and do to me.
I am a warrior, and there is power in my tongue.
I can build up or I can pull down.
I can kill or can give birth with the power of my words.
There is power in my tongue.

But I will use this tongue to praise You, Lord.
I will use my words to exalt Your holy name.
I will lash at the devil's schemes.
I will use the authority I have in words.

I will speak to my mountains and watch them crumble.
I will speak to the barren land and watch it bear.
I will speak to the depress and watch them cheer.
Yes, there is power in my tongue.

There was a world of iniquity in this tongue,
But You sanctified it by the blood of the Lamb.
I will now use it to bring You honour.
I will use it against the demonic forces,
I will pull down strongholds,
I will tie up the strong man,
with the authority of my words.
There is power in my tongue.

Trampling

Who knew trampling could be so rewarding?
Who knew trampling could be so fulfilling?
Who knew trampling is powerful?
Who knew there is authority in trampling?
So, let's trample! Trample! Trample!
We're trampling.

Who knew trampling could be so rewarding?
Who knew trampling could be so fulfilling?
Who knew trampling is powerful?
Who knew there is authority in trampling?
So, trample! Let's trample!
Trample on the enemy. Trample him!

Who knew I can trample on snakes?
Who knew I can trample on serpents?
Who knew I can trample on scorpions?
Who knew? Who knew I had that authority?
So, trample! Let's trample!
Let's trample on the enemy.

Who knew we can trample on Satan's head?
Who knew that the devil is under our feet?
Who knew that the wicked will be trampled down?

Let's trample! Let's trample!
Let's trample on the enemy.

Chapter 4

Be Encouraged

Above and Beyond

Commit thy ways onto the Lord, and He will bring them
to pass.
Submit thyself onto the Lord, and He shall lift you up.
He will grant the desires of your heart
Above and beyond.

I hold You to Your Word.
It's my currency, Lord.
Once You uttered it once, I claim it.
I will stretch and train my faith.
I activate Your promises
Above and beyond.

Your Words ring in my ears and establish in my heart: *I
love you, I am your God.
I will honour you, I will be with you,
I will protect you.*

I hold unto to those words, Lord,
Above and beyond.

I wait on You, Lord,
For You, above and beyond.

Looking unto You

Often, I am not sure where the wind will blow.
Sometimes, I am caught in the whirlwind, drowning in
tears and broken.
The devil is on the attack, and he's using my love.
I am heartbroken and confused.

Rest is evading me; food has no taste
My mind is weighed down, and it's dark all around.
But I look unto You, from whence come my help.

You promised me elevation, Lord,
But here I am at the bottom.
You promised me promotion, Lord,
But here I am demoted.
You promised I am the head, Lord,
But I stand all alone, no one to lead
and no one to follow.
But I look unto You, Lord, from whence come my help.

I will encourage myself in the Lord.
Even when I feel broken, I will look unto You, Lord.
When I am lost, I will find my way home in You.
When I am confused, I will turn to You for clarity.
I will trust You.

When You say promoted, promoted it will be.

When You say lead, lead I will—even standing alone, I will lead.

I will walk in the spirit, I will rejoice in Your Word.

I will look unto my God because I don't need to understand it all.

Be Encouraged!

Be encouraged by the Lord and in the power of His might.
If you don't have Him, you have nothing.
Put your confidence in Him.
Trust in His holiness and in the power of His Word.
If you don't have Him, you have nothing.

Encourage yourself in the Lord.
Be encouraged by His promises.
Seek His face for clarification.
Seek His Word for direction.
Because if you don't have Him, you have nothing.

He is there; just call on Him, trust Him.
Peace and joy will flow through your soul.
Blessings and health will pour down your core.
If you don't have Him, you have nothing.

Be encouraged.
It is just a test to bring you into perfection.
You will survive this storm.
Don't be distracted by the whirlwind.
Focus on Him,
Because if we don't have Him, we have nothing.
Be encouraged!

$\mathcal{I}$ Have Not

No, I have not arrived.
No, I have not figured it all out.
No, I am not perfect; I am quite flawed.
Nor have I overcome every one of my vices.

I am a work in progress.
I am a diamond in the rough.
But I have faith in the Diamond Cutter.
I am on the road to redemption.

No, I have not arrived;
There are still sins to overcome.
Sometimes I want to pull the trigger,
but I won't give the devil the pleasure.

I am a work in progress,
Unrefined gold.
But I have faith in the Goldsmith.
He's putting me through the fire,
To purify me into pure gold.

No, I have not arrived.
Sometimes I feel lost in this world,
Looking for crumbs to find my way home,
Circling the same path, making no progress.
But I'm fitted with a GPS.
My navigator is the Creator.
He will steer me down the best path for my life.
He will guide me home.

You may be broken in parts,
Scattered on the floor.
Put your faith in the Jesus.
He will find your pieces,
And finish what He started.
We were bought with His blood,
Redeemed from death.
He's working on our perfecting.

Thorn in My Side

I stand and preach,
Singing a lovely tune.
I kneel, weeping, humbling to my King.
I exhort and encourage.
I am well respected.

But behind closed doors,
I have this thorn in me.
My blood is seeping on the floor.

I walk with kings;
I am viewed as royalty.
I can heal the sick
And have faith to raise the dead.
I am confident in who I am.
I can overcome any feat.

But I have a secret,
A thorn deep within.
Tears are rolling down my cheeks.

I can speak in many tongues.
I can move mountains.
I can slay demons, upset principalities.
But I have a secret I will scream:
His grace is sufficient for me!

God-Inspired Wisdom

Day 1 … When you know the Holy Spirit has deposited something in your spirit, write it down, meditate on it, run with it. Don't let the devil steal it from you.

> Then the Lord said to me, "Write my answer plainly on tablets, so that a runner can carry the correct message to others. This vision is for a future time. It describes the end, and it will be fulfilled. If it seems slow in coming, wait patiently, for it will surely take place. It will not be delayed." (Habakkuk 2:2–3 NLT)

Day 2 … We will go through seasons of difficulty, but don't let it get you down. Feed your faith; feed your hope. If you need to listen to that one sermon over and over or read that one scripture daily to remind you of what God promised, do it. Kill the enemy's chatter with the Word of God. Why feed doubt and discouragement when you can feed your confidence and be encouraged? Strengthen your faith. Surround yourself with the love and peace of

God. Put that word on repeat until it changes you, until the promise is fulfilled.

> Finally, believers, whatever is true, whatever is honourable and worthy of respect, whatever is right and confirmed by God's word, whatever is pure and wholesome, whatever is lovely and brings peace, whatever is admirable and of good repute; if there is any excellence, if there is anything worthy of praise, think continually on these things [center your mind on them, and implant them in your heart]. (Philippians 4:8 AMP)

Day 3 ... Preach to yourself. Remind the inner man of what God said. Encourage yourself. Find that positive thing to say. Speak the language of God.

> Why are you in despair, O my soul? And why are you restless and disturbed within me? Hope in God and wait expectantly for Him, for I shall again praise Him, The help of my [sad] countenance and my God. (Psalm 43:5 AMP)

Day 4. ... Be careful how much weight you give to your emotions. Our emotions are often fickle; we could be sad one minute and happy the next. Annoy one minute, rejoicing the next. Just like a flick of a switch, our emotions can change. Therefore, Praise God even when you don't feel like it. Do what you know is right, even when you don't feel like it.

> But Jesus didn't trust them, because He knew human nature. No one needed to tell Him what mankind is really like. (John 2:24–25 NLT)

Day 5 … When you have a dream, or a desire that you just can't shake, even though it seems impossible. People say it's a fairy-tale, they laugh at you, but you just can't let it go. Know that God may have deposited it there, work towards it, and keep trusting Him despite how impossible it may appear. He is the God of the impossible.

> Take delight in the Lord, and He will give you your heart's desires. Commit everything you do to the Lord. Trust Him, and He will help you. (Psalm 37:4 NLT)

> But Jesus beheld them, and said unto them, with men this is impossible; but with God all things are possible. (Matthew 19:26 KJV)

Day 6 … When the hour is dark and you don't understand what is happening, it doesn't align with the promise or His Word, and your confidence may be shattered. You may be overwhelmed and confused, but keep your eyes on God. If you hold unto Him, you will come out on top without scars. But hold tight to your confidence. Don't let the devil steal it. That dark hour could be eleven days or forty years. The choice is yours.

> Let us hold tightly without wavering to the hope we affirm, for God can be trusted to keep his promise. (Hebrews 10:23 NLT)

> So do not throw away this confident trust in the Lord. Remember the great reward it brings you! Patient endurance is what you need now, so that you will continue to do God's will. Then you will receive all that he has promised. (Hebrews 10:35–36 NLT)

Day 7 ... That talent, that ability you have—use it. Use them all! God distributed talents according to His wisdom, and He expects a return on what He gave to us. Don't wait for the "right" time. Today may be the day, before it is too late. The enemy will discourage you and bring excuses, but put that talent to work at every opportunity that crosses your path. Fast, pray, and put your talent to work.

> Then you should have invested my money with the bankers, and at my coming I would have received what was my own with interest. So, take the talent away from him and give it to the one who has the ten talents. For to everyone who has will more be given, and he will be furnished richly so that he will have an abundance;

but from the one who does not have, even what he does have will be taken away. And throw the good-for-nothing servant into the outer darkness; there will be weeping and grinding of teeth. (Matthew 25:27–30 AMPC)

Printed in the United States
By Bookmasters